Modern Railways Pictorial ANNUAL 1985

Above:
The majority of photographs taken in Cornwall depict the summer scene and studies of winter trains amid leafless trees are far from commonplace. Early on a bleak February morning in 1982 the 07.40 Penzance-Liverpool Lime Street is powered towards Penadlake viaduct on the climb to Liskeard by Class 50 No 50.043 *Eagle*. *Brian Morrison*

£4.95

On an attractive stretch of the Dartford Loop line between Bexley and Crayford, Class 33/0 No 33.056 *The Burma Star* heads eastwards with a very mixed air-braked freight from the London Midland Region to Sheerness via Kensington Olympia and Sidcup on a cloudless 22 June 1981. *Brian Morrison*

Modern Railways Pictorial
ANNUAL 1985
Edited by Brian Morrison

LONDON
IAN ALLAN LTD

First published 1984

ISBN 0 7110 1444 2

Published by Ian Allan Ltd, Shepperton, Surrey; and printed by Ian Allan Printing Ltd at their works at Coombelands in Runnymede, England.

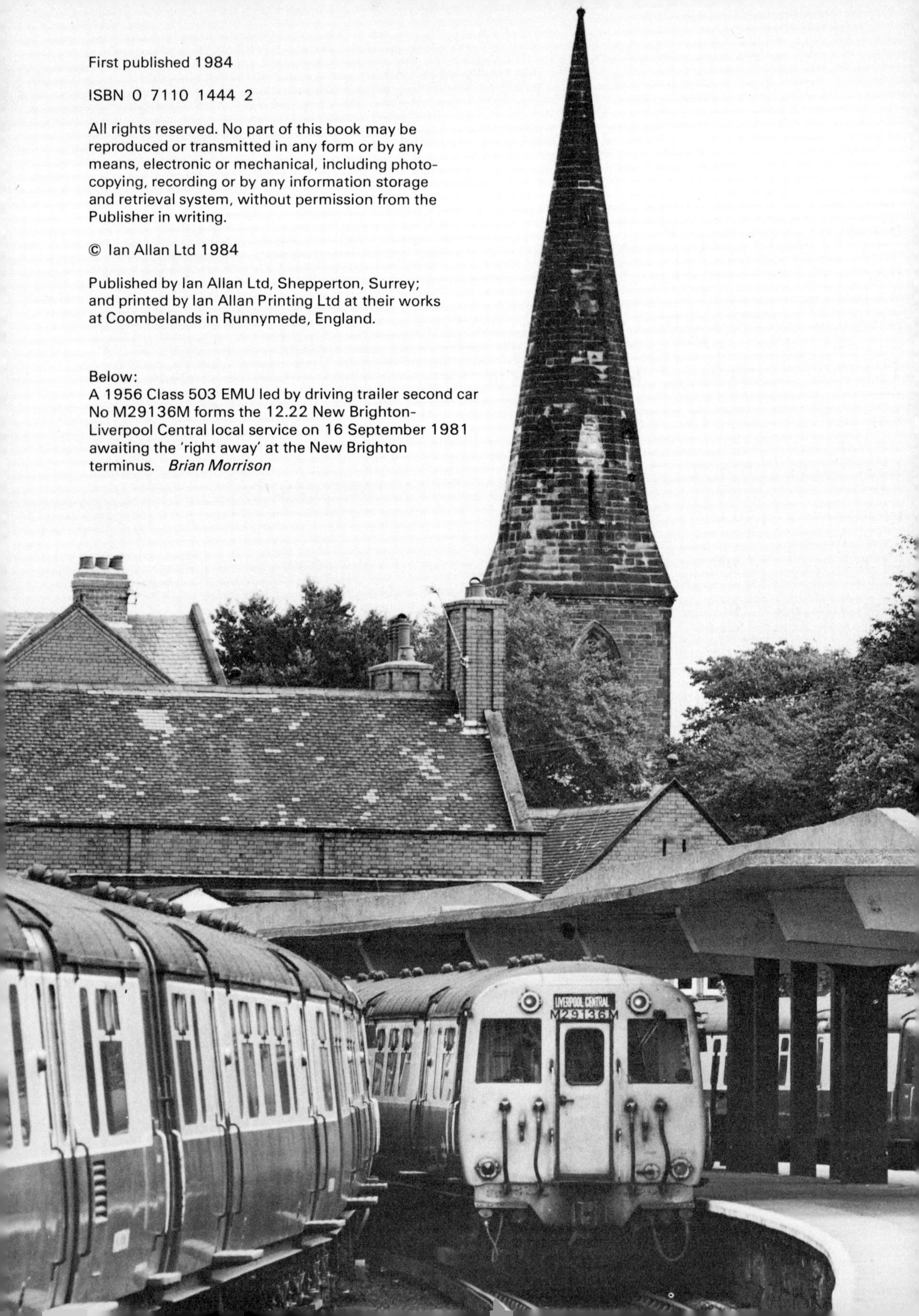

Below:
A 1956 Class 503 EMU led by driving trailer second car No M29136M forms the 12.22 New Brighton-Liverpool Central local service on 16 September 1981 awaiting the 'right away' at the New Brighton terminus. *Brian Morrison*

Contents

Cover:
An oily, travel-stained 'Peak' contrasts with the summer holiday beach scene as it hauls the 06.38 Leeds-Paignton past the red cliffs of Coryton's Cove, near Dawlish, in July 1980. Arrival at Paignton is scheduled for 13.43. *Brian Morrison*

Shoeburyness via Tilbury

All photographs by **Brian Morrison**

That the present day services on the old London, Tilbury & Southend Railway lines are some of the most under-photographed in the country, there is no doubt. The reasons, one imagines, range from a sparcity of scenery to an overabundance of the somewhat dull looking Class 302 EMU. True, but there is still quite a lot of freight traffic to be seen east of Thames Haven Junction and, even from Pitsea to the terminus of Shoeburyness, the numerous units that ply back and forth from Fenchurch Street are capable of being recorded in a setting that is quite scenic. It is hoped that this selection of photographs that concentrate on the line from Barking via Tilbury to Shoeburyness may help to redress the balance of photographic coverage on the line, at least to some extent.

Top left:
The high rise flats of Barking can be seen on the hazy horizon of a July evening in 1983 as the 17.26 Fenchurch Street-Tilbury Riverside commuter service passes the yards to the west of Ripple Lane formed of two Class 502 EMUs with No 248 leading.

Bottom left:
Between Barking and Dagenham Dock stations lies the depot and yards of Ripple Lane, from where a reasonable number of freight services emanate; these consist mainly of oil tanks for the oil refineries at Coryton and Thames Haven, Cartics from the Ford Motor Works at Dagenham and Freightliners from the Ripple Lane terminus. Nicely captured in echelon at Ripple Lane on 26 April 1983 are Class 37 No 37.162 with a haul of tanks and Class 47/0 No 47.006 with a string of empty flats, both of which await the passing of an eight-car Class 302 formation headed by No 302.265 forming the 16.10 Shoeburyness-Fenchurch Street.

Right:
An unlikely combination of grazing cattle and pylon-infested fields form the background to the 17.40 Shoeburyness-Fenchurch Street as it passes between Dagenham Dock and Ripple lane. The Class 308/302 formation is led by No 308.319.

Below:
On 8 September 1982 the Ripple Lane yards look entirely different with a rake of oil tanks waiting to leave behind Class 31/1s Nos 31.137 and 31.223 and a Freightliner being propelled back into the Freightliner terminus to the rear by Class 08 shunter No 08.627.

Above:
A heavy load of tanks from Thames Haven approaches Dagenham Dock on 4 August 1983 hauled by Class 37 No 37.001. Most of the freight traffic on this line is inter-Regional and this train is bound for the London Midland Region. On the right Class 47 No 47.006 awaits clearance with a rake of Toleman's cartics loaded with Ford products from the plant on the left.

Below:
Approaching Rainham, the 17.22 Fenchurch Street-Pitsea commuter service passes a loaded cartic of Ford Sierras and Fiestas from the Dagenham plant on the right of the photograph. The train is made up from four-car Class 302 No 302.281 and newly reformed three-car Class 308/2 No 308.994.

Above right:
With a haul of 100-ton bogie oil tanks, Class 37 No 37.263 runs along the esturial levels towards Purfleet with a trip working from Ripple Lane to Thames Haven.

Below right:
In addition to the line that loops around the northern banks of the River Thames travelling via Tilbury, a more direct route to the south Essex coast runs from Barking through Upminster and rejoins the Tilbury route at Pitsea. A connecting link between the two operates with a shuttle service between Upminster and Grays via Ockendon; this is inevitably a Class 302 electric unit. Glinting in the cold winter sunshine of a January morning in 1981, unit No 294 has just left Grays with the 10.40 for Upminster.

000

294

Above:
Tilbury Riverside station is a terminus formed in the lower apex of a triangle off the line between Tilbury Town and East Tilbury and through services are obliged to reverse on leaving. Awaiting for the driver to walk from the far end of the train is Class 302 unit No 243 forming the 10.35 Fenchurch Street-Shoeburyness.

Below:
A number of local services do not travel the full length of the line from Fenchurch Street to Shoeburyness, terminating instead at Tilbury Riverside where a six-line siding is provided for stock superfluous to daytime or weekend rostas. Class 302 EMUs Nos 240, 290, 299 and 248 are the occupants on a winter Saturday afternoon in 1981.

Above:
With the chimneys of the Mobil oil refinery at Coryton and parts of the industrial Canvey Island on the skyline, a 12-car formation of Class 302 stock crosses the Hadleigh Marshes on 3 August 1983 as the 16.21 Shoeburyness-Fenchurch Street service. This is a distant view from a roadside brought into prominence through a 180mm f2.8 Nikkor lens fitted to a Nikon FM2 camera.

Below:
A scene at Pitsea where the lines that part at Barking reconverge for the final part of their journeys. Trains from Fenchurch Street via Upminster and Tilbury respectively make their obligatory Pitsea stop on their services to Shoeburyness and Southend Central. The leading four-car units are Nos 302.281 and 263, the latter still to receive a class number prefix and marker lights when photographed in August 1983.

302
302

Above left:
The nameboards at this station read 'Benfleet for Canvey Island'. Afternoon shoppers from Southend alight from the 16.51 Shoeburyness-Fenchurch Street which is formed of two Class 302 units with No 302.302 at the rear.

Below left:
Between Chalkwell and Leigh-on-Sea the Shoeburyness line hugs the banks of the Thames Estuary where day trippers and the occasional holidaymaker use the limited facilities of the beaches. Leaving Leigh-on-Sea station and passing almost a shanty town of beach structures, the 15.20 Southend Central-Fenchurch Street is led by Class 302 EMU No 231 with sister unit No 238 completing the eight-car formation.

Above:
Further along the estuary wall near to Chalkwell, Class 302 No 302.262 forms the 14.45 from the London terminus to Southend Central.

Below:
The 13.10 ex-Fenchurch Street rolls to a halt in Shoeburyness on a dull January day in 1981. The track here at the time looked like a rubbish tip!

302
301

Left:
A striking illustration of the differing results that can be obtained from the same location without even moving one's feet! A previous photograph was taken through a 35mm wide-angle lens whereas this one was exposed from exactly the same spot but with the camera fitted with a 180mm telephoto optic. Here the 15.59 Thorpe Bay-Fenchurch Street is made up of Class 302s Nos 302.270 and 302.301.

Below:
Chalkwell pier? Holidaymakers look out over the Thames Estuary as Class 302 No 302.236 passes behind them with the 15.58 from Shoeburyness to Fenchurch Street.

Photoguide 'Phunnies'

All photographs by **Les Nixon** unless otherwise indicated

The MRP Photoguide series, since its inception in the June 1982 issue, has taken rather a serious look at various aspects of railway photography but for the first *MRP Annual* we will take a more lighthearted view of our hobby.

A few moments reflection brings to mind a number of events which although perhaps not particularly funny at the time, seem quite hilarious today. One of my earliest recollections goes back to schooldays when I was already dabbling, albeit unsuccessfully, with developer and fixer in a darkened kitchen. Needless to say schoolfriends were keen to avail themselves of a cut price D&P service; and one film entrusted to my care was the first a friend had taken at Crewe — pictures of unrebuilt 'Patriots', 'Scots' and the diesel-electric prototypes Nos 10000 and 10001. Development produced nothing but a totally black string of negatives; there wasn't even the trace of an image. My processing was not so good but surely not that bad! Surprisingly my friend wasn't at all disappointed by the news, he simply commented 'Ah well, I didn't expect them to turn out, I had already had a quick look at the film and I couldn't see anything either'!

Then there was the usual disastrous effects of 'developing' films in fixer or even just plain water and exposing 35mm films twice. Economical photography perhaps but hardly to be recommended!

Among more recent experiences was the development of a film exposed during a visit to Scotland in the late 1960s. The film was duly developed and I was very pleased with the results — almost perfect negatives. The film was washed and hung to dry from the back of a chair. Along came the family cat who promptly used the film for claw sharpening practice! Those scratches defied all attempts of restoration work and the ensuing feline persecution would have been a credit to a Tom and Jerry cartoon!

Another mishap followed yet another visit North of the Border (why did it always seem to be Scottish films?). Again the film was carefully processed and placed in the sink to wash. It continues to be my practice to wash films by using a constant stream of tap water along with a simple overflow device — a foolproof system one would think. Not at all! On this occasion my concentration lapsed and instead of a continuous flow of *cold* water . . . I am sure by now you have guessed the rest! Thirty minutes later all I had was the film base and distorted gelatin floating on the surface of very hot water. Of course I still maintain that those pictures were among the best I have ever taken!

On a totally different theme my first experiments with movie cameras were equally embarrassing. At the time it seemed obvious to build on the experience of still photography and I knew that certain pictures are best in a vertical rather than a horizontal format. It wasn't until I eagerly projected my first movie film that I realised that this certainly wasn't an option in movie photography! For a long time I used to think that a photographer would eventually become so experienced that he would be able to anticipate and effectively deal with just about every problem but I find that I am still learning after all these years. Within the last few months I have, yet again, spent a day's photography with no film in the camera! For black and white work I occasionally find that I have the wrong film in the camera for the day's photography — FP4 isn't much good on a dull winter's day. Recently a partially exposed FP4 roll film was wound off on to the take-up spool and a mental note made to rewind the film in the darkroom to make use of the unexposed frames. (With roll film you cannot of course rewind into a cassette as you can with a 35mm camera). Surprise, surprise, some two weeks later the roll film had not been rewound it was re-loaded directly into the camera, only to find that the whole wind on mechanism then jammed solid.

Another amusing episode concerns a photographer who took his car at low tide on to Morecambe Bay sands to obtain some potential prize winning telephoto cross shots. The car slowly settled, became immobile, and became well submerged by high tide.

Talking of cars, I wonder if you are in the habit of keeping your cameras in the car boot overnight? Certainly it used to be my practice until I found that in winter I was often losing the first pictures of the day because of condensation on the lens.

The moral of the story? — if a friend tells you that every picture he takes is a winner — we all know better.

Above:
Believe it or not this amusing picture was not planned. The apparent collision between the DMU and the brakevan came as a complete surprise when the film was developed. Class 127 DMU forming a St Pancras-Bedford service passes vacant sidings at Cricklewood on 21 May 1977

Below:
Perhaps the most amusing contrast on British Rail. No doubt one of the original drivers of *Lion* would have crouched behind his steed had he spied a new fangled 1980s DMU passing by on the next track. A Class 104 DMU with a Manchester (Victoria)-Southport service passes *Lion* on proving trials for the Rainhill celebrations at Burscough on 12 May 1980.

Left:
Is this a picture of BR's long term solution to its economic crisis? It certainly seems as though a double-deck train with loaded MGR wagons on top of an HST was passing Dearne Colliery near Cudworth on 16 September 1982.

Below left:
A novel triple header! Class 40 No 40.075 leads Class 76 No 26020 and narrow gauge steam locomotive *The Earl* past Mossley near Stalybridge en route for Rainhill on 20 May 1980.

Right:
A photograph that now produces a smile — but it didn't at the time. As the 18.40 for Liverpool Street leaves Norwich behind Class 37 No 37.017 the photographer is completed 'bowled' by the appearance from behind him of an '08' shunter marshalling empty stock. *Brian Morrison*

Below:
Was the photographer in 'drag' to get this picture of a Class 101 DMU forming the 12.20 Ely-Norwich at Ely on 26 February 1980? The view from the Ladies' Waiting Room was certainly better than the one from the Gents!

Above:
Amusing in retrospect! Double-headed Class 50s passing through Sheffield are exceedingly rare and your photographer fell into the classic trap of trying to take too many pictures. A very ordinary telephoto picture was obtained (which barely shows the second locomotive) at the expense of this standard lens shot. The leading locomotive was almost out of view by the time the shutter on the second camera could be released. Class 50s Nos 50.045 *Achilles* and 50.042 *Triumph* head the 12.37 Leeds-Cardiff through Dore on 27 May 1982.

Left:
Watched by an elderly relative a young enthusiast searches in vain for No 673 in his 1980 Ian Allan *ABC British Rail Motive Power Pocket book*! Beauty and the beast (I will leave you to decide which is which!) in the form of Class 25 No 25.217 and 'Spinner' 4-2-2 No 673 at Manchester Victoria on 28 May 1980.

Above right:
A Class 56 bites its own tail! On its very first day in service No 56.084 runs round its load at Bentley Colliery on 30 October 1980 only to discover — too late — that the end hopper hadn't cleared the crossing! *Colin Marsden*

Right:
Another 'piggyback' picture! Appearing to be giving 'junior' a ride, Class 414/3 2HAP No 6065 leads two 4VEP units forming an ECS working for Selhurst Depot while behind Class 427 4VEG No 7902 takes the 08.40 from Bognor Regis on to its Victoria destination. The scene is between Three Bridges and Gatwick Airport. *Brian Morrison*

6065
04

SR DC Electric Locomotives

Colin J. Marsden

Electric locomotives are normally considered a relatively modern innovation, but the story of the SR's electric locomotive traction dates back to the late 1930s when Mr A. Raworth, the Southern Railway electrical engineer, received permission for the construction of three DC locomotives, primarily for freight operation. After Oliver Bulleid, the Chief Mechanical Engineer, saw the proposals he insisted that a mixed traffic locomotive was required and produced amended drawings for a Co-Co locomotive. An interesting feature of this design was a pantograph carried amidships on the roof, which was intended for use in yards where the presence of a third rail would have been dangerous to staff. During the early stages of design a problem was foreseen with the continuity of the power supply to the locomotive when operating from the third rail pick-up system because there were so many gaps in the existing conductor rails, particularly in point and crossing work. This problem had not been previously encountered, because on EMU trains a number of pick-up shoes were provided over the length of the train which was usually far longer than any gap in the conductor rail. To overcome this problem a booster unit was installed in the form of a flywheel generator which enabled power to be supplied even when the locomotive lost contact with the third rail.

Locomotive construction was awarded to Ashford and the first of the fleet appeared in 1941 carrying the SR number CC1; this was followed in 1943 by No CC2. The war years contributed to the third locomotive not emerging until after nationalisation in 1948 and numbered 20003 (numbers CC1/2 becoming 20001/2).

The locomotives were normally used on the Central Division London-Brighton line and some sidings on the route were equipped for the overhead power pick-up system. After a decline in freight traffic the locomotives found use on Victoria-Newhaven boat trains and during the 1960s were favourite motive power for the Region's Royal Trains.

Although under the BR numerical classification the three examples became Class 70, the class prefix numbers were never carried. All three locomotives were withdrawn in 1969 as non-standard and cut up.

However the story of Southern Region electric locomotives was far from over, as under the 1955 modernisation plans, which included the electrification of the Kent Coast main line, a fleet of 24 dual pick-up 750V DC electric locomotives was authorised and constructed at the BR Workshops, Doncaster. These production examples differed considerably from the three SR designed prototypes, being mounted on a Bo-Bo style underframe with the major design emphasis being placed on power/weight ratio. The booster system was retained from the SR locomotives to ensure power continuation over section gaps. Much of the locomotive design, particularly in the mechanical section, was attributable to continental influences, following the British Transport Commission's study of continental electric locomotives. The features adopted included springborne traction motors, SLM flexible drives and a bogie type based on SLM practice and constructed under licence at the BR workshops, Doncaster. The design incorporated the conventional bogie central pivot for power weight transfer and also secondary suspension. The total power output for these new main line locomotives was 2,552hp with a total operational weight of around 77 tons, comparing favourably with the prototypes weighing 100 tons and giving 1,470hp.

Another feature retained from the Raworth/Bulleid locomotive was the central roof-mounted pantograph for yard pick-up. Because the locomotives were designed as a replacement to steam traction, steam heating was not fitted; instead the comparatively new electric train heat (ETH) system was installed and for some years this caused problems with the diagramming of stock on the SR.

The locomotives gave superb service with a high rate of reliability and availability. Two duties they will always be associated with were the 'Golden Arrow' and 'Night Ferry' services. They were all allocated to the South Eastern Division and usually maintained at Ashford or Stewarts Lane depots.

By the mid-1960s some of the locomotives were surplus to requirements but were saved from the torch by the need for 10 high powered electro-diesels for the Waterloo-Bournemouth electrification. So 10 of the fleet were rebuilt from 1966 at Crewe Works, but that is another story.

Under the numerical numbering system the BTC-designed locomotives became Class 71.

Above:
The first of the Raworth/Bulleid 'Booster' locomotives — No CC1 painted in SR green with yellow whisker strips on the front. It will be noted that a two-character headcode position was provided, later to be plated over in favour of lamps/discs, only to be resurrected in the 1960s when a two positioned wind up indicator was fitted. No CC1 approaches Merstham with a down goods on 5 December 1941. *BR*

Below:
The third locomotive of the type was largely different from the first two with a more slab front end and the vacuum pipe being buffer beam mounted. Painted in BR livery No 20003 is seen when new in the works yard at Brighton with the DC pantograph in the raised position. *Colin J. Marsden collection*

Above:
Approaching Three Bridges No 20002 hauls a Newhaven-Victoria boat train on 12 April 1958. It was on this route that the locomotives saw most use after their displacement from freight traffic.
John N. Faulkner

Below:
Displaying its distinctive 'Night Ferry' headboard, No E5000 hauls the London bound service during the summer of 1960. This locomotive was renumbered E5024 in December 1962 and was eventually rebuilt in 1966 as an electro-diesel. *Colin J. Marsden collection*

Right:
During 1959 a number of training and test trips were operated on the SED for the majority of drivers had not come across 'booster' electric traction before. No E5001 with nose-mounted ETH jumper passes Dunton Green during June 1959 with an up electrical test train. *Derek Cross*

Below right:
In pristine condition No E5009 complete with red body side band and painted in BR locomotive green livery, passes Shortlands Junction with an up vans train bound for Hither Green in 1960.
Colin J. Marsden collection

Above:
With a characteristic 'Golden Arrow' headboard mounted on the upper lamp brackets, purposely provided for headboard fixture, No E5007 passes Petts Wood with the southbound working on 1 October 1968. *John Cooper-Smith*

Below:
In addition to operating the 'Golden Arrow' and 'Night Ferry' duties Class 71s were normally employed on freight operations to and from the channel ports to the international freight terminal at Hither Green. A southbound freight formed of a German owned ferry van and three BR vehicles approaches St Mary Cray on 26 August 1976 headed by No 71.006.
Brian Morrison

Above right:
After the class were deemed non-standard during the autumn of 1976, the complete fleet were stored at various locations and finally withdrawn en bloc in November 1977. No 71.011 stands awaiting its fate at Stewarts Lane depot in mid-1977. *Colin J. Marsden*

Below right:
Last resting place. Awaiting cutting-up on Doncaster Works scrapline on 19 August 1979 are Nos 71.009, 71.014, 71.011, 71.013, 71.004 and 74.010.
Brian Morrison

71011

71009

The Old and the New Orders at St Pancras

All photographs by **Brian Morrison**

For more years than most of us care to remember, the traffic to and from St Pancras has been in the hands of the 1Co-Co1 'Peaks' and the Rolls-Royce-engined Class 127 diesel multiple-units with the occasional Class 47 putting in an appearance. Seemingly almost overnight the InterCity 125s have taken over nearly all the locomotive-hauled expresses and the faithful but aged Class 127s have been usurped by the appearance at last of the new Class 317 electric units on the surburban services. This feature illustrates the changes taking place with both the old motive power and the new running side by side. All the photographs were taken on 24 June 1983 with a 35mm Nikon FM2 camera fitted with either a 35mm or a 50mm f1.4 Nikkor lens.

Below:
The 10.43 for Bedford Midland awaits the 'off' at platform 1 formed of a Class 317 EMU No 317.334.

Right:
One train that must remain locomotive hauled at this time is the travelling post office. With an early morning arrival of an overnight TPO, Class 45/1 No 45.103 stands at the St Pancras buffer stops.

45103

E20
ST PANCRAS
M77081

43107
Inter-City 125

Above left:
The 11.13 for Bedford Midland is still in the hands of a Derby-built Class 127 four-car unit with driving motor brake second class car No M51599 leading. An earlier departure is rostered for a Class 317 electric unit which occupies the country end of the same platform.

Above:
Morning main line arrivals whose respective ages span nearly two decades share platforms under the superb St Pancras train shed.

Left:
With its power car number 43107 now displayed in a central position on the front end, a Class 254 Inter-City unit moves the 12.10 to Nottingham away from the station.

Above:
A forlorn 'Peak' — No 45.112 — joins the ranks of the unemployed as Class 253 InterCity unit No 253.026 glides past the famous St Pancras gasholders forming the 12.30 Sheffield-St Pancras.

Below:
Brush Class 47/4 No 47.426 has just backed out of St Pancras station after arrival with a parcels train and manoeuvres in order to reach the Cambridge Street fuelling lines. Passing on the down 'fast' is a Class 253 HST forming the 15.30 to Sheffield and losing the race on the down 'slow' is Class 317 No 317.307 with a very late running local service for Bedford Midland caused by a temporary power failure further down the line.

Below:
For over a year the Class 317 EMUs for the St Pancras-Bedford services ('bedpan' units as they were christened by the media!) stood idle in sidings awaiting an agreement upon manning levels between union and BR management. At last they started to move and driver training could commence. Unit No 317.321 is here so engaged prior to commencement of the takeover from the ageing DMU fleet.
Adrian Chamberlain

Out in the Cold

Words and photographs by **Brian Morrison**

It is a well known fact that a fall of snow can transform a mundane scene into one that is very attractive. It can be exhilarating to play winter sports or indeed any pursuit that keeps the circulation surging. Railway photography is not one of them!

In wintertime trains have a habit of being late and of not being nearly as prolific as during the summer months. The cold has a way of permeating through the soles of one's boots and, despite thick socks, seems to creep up the legs as though they were acting as a form of blotting paper. Some form of exercise would probably solve the problem but the odds are that it will be during that short jog along the road that the train will pass! So one stands in icy solitude peering into the distance and hoping that it won't be too long before the train arrives and the photographer can at last return to the car and turn the heater up full blast.

Of course it isn't just cold discomfort that is a problem. Another is getting to the snowbound location in the first place: hitting black ice on a downhill country road in Cumbria; encountering a quite unnerving 'white-out' on the coal road near Ribblehead and having a hike in a blizzard to locate a willing farmer with a tractor to pull the car from a ditch; being unaware of a frozen gully across a snow covered field near Glenfinnan and receiving a rush of ice cold water over the top of the left boot; wondering why the car wouldn't start after a lengthy session and finding that the petrol had frozen in the carburettor! All these little distractions have happened over the past few winters and, no doubt, more are yet to come as, in the warmth of one's home looking at the results, it all seems worthwhile. A sincere thank you, anyway, to the inventor of thermal clothing.

Below:
With a haul of vans for Carlisle, Class 85 electric locomotive No 85.002 races through Grayrigg on 9 February 1983. The Cumbrian mountains are the backcloth to this Christmas card scene.

Above:
On 10 February 1983, Class 47/4 No 47.545 is making good use of its electric train heating as it leaves Ulverston with the 11.15 Barrow-in-Furness to Liverpool Lime Street.

Below:
A heavy fall of snow on 9 December 1981 transforms the cutting near New Eltham on the Dartford Loop line into a winter wonderland. Class 415/1 4EPB No 5154 keeps time with the 10.53 Dartford-Charing Cross via Sidcup.

Above:
On 16 December 1981 the snow around Marsden lay deep and crisp and even. With the low sun casting an almost pink hue to the attractive scene, ETH fitted Class 47 No 47.436 heads westwards with the 09.50

Below:
Although photographed as late in the year as 22 March, snow still abounds in the Lune Valley as the 13.23 Edinburgh-Taunton train whistles through headed by Class 87 Bo-Bo No 87.001 *Royal Scot*.

Above left:
In the big freeze of January 1982 even the familiar scene in Clapham cutting took on a new look and Waterloo Control was forced to dispense with its timetables and run trains where and when possible. On the left a Class 423 4VEP No 7706 waits for a path into Clapham Junction at the rear of a service from Guildford while Class 508 No 508.010 passes on the down 'slow' with a Waterloo-Hampton Court train.

Below left:
Crossing at Newtonmore on 12 February 1979. Class 25/1 No 25.065 heads southwards with a short freight train bound for Perth while one of the original Class 25s, No 25.002, passes and makes for Dingwall with an equally short haul. Both these locomotives are now withdrawn from stock.

Above:
Loaded with stone from Ribblehead quarry, Class 25/2 No 25.161 waits in a blizzard to take her train away to Skipton.

Below:
Not long after the previous photograph was taken there were problems that arose when it was found impossible to identify the road from the ditch on either side and the inevitable happened! An obliging local farmer uses his tractor to haul the photographer's car back on to the thickly snow covered roadway.

A superb winter scene at Marsden, just into ER territory at the eastern end of Standedge Tunnel. With heavy snow clinging to the foliage and covering the siding in the foreground, Class 37 No 37.141 (then of Thornaby) hauls a rake a bogie tanks towards the tunnel — and the LMR — on 16 December 1981. *Les Nixon*

The first snow of the winter invariably brings out the photographers, particularly when the fall is followed by sunshine. On 12 December 1981 the 13.19 Morecambe-Leeds service is seen at Borwick, a few miles east of Carnforth, formed of a BR Derby Class 108 four-car set. *Les Nixon*

Above:
Taken from the station overbridge in a temperature of around -8°C with a Force 6 'breeze' coming off the Irish Sea and across Duddon Sands, Kirkby-in-Furness station was as bleak a location as one could imagine when this photograph of Class 47/0 No 47.224 was taken in February 1983 hauling a Lakeland Colliery-Fiddlers Ferry MGR.

Below:
Amid a winter landscape Class 45/0 'Peak' No 45.070 scampers through Settle Junction with just four coaches that make up the 10.00 Carlisle-Leeds. The train has travelled through the worst weather that the Settle & Carlisle route could offer and will now gradually leave the snow behind as the mountains recede in the background. The tracks on the left are the 'Little LNWR' route to Carlisle via Barrow-in-Furness and Workington.

Right:
What may have been the 07.00 Newcastle-Bristol Temple Meads train is hauled by 'Peak' No 45.125 at Vigo on the Lickey Bank on 12 December 1981.
Geoff Dowling

Below:
A combination of good luck and fine skill secured this exceptional photograph on 23 April 1982. 'Slim Jim' Class 33 No 33.209 leaving Northfleet freight terminal in Kent with gypsum empties bound for Tonbridge and eventually Mountfield; while above Class 33/0 No 33.048 hauls a rake of cement Presflos from Strood to the WR on the main line. *Les Bertram*

Right:
On 17 September 1983, Ian Allan Ltd organised a special train from Waterloo to the Severn Valley Railway via Reading, Oxford and Birmingham. Two named 'Cromptons' were provided by Eastleigh and here No 33.025 *Sultan* leads No 33.027 *Earl Mountbatten of Burma* through Radley.
C. W. Wilkinson

Last Years of the 'Marys'

All photographs by **Brian Morrison**

The Southern Region's Class 405 4SUB units, or 'Mary's as they were affectionately nicknamed by both railwaymen and enthusiasts alike, were real 'old ladies of the road' on the Southern's surburban routes. Introduced originally between 1948 and 1951, many of them received underframes and bogies salvaged from earlier generations of withdrawn EMU stock. Inroads into the once numerous class have been made for a number of years but the introduction of the Class 508 resulted in a particularly large batch being taken out of service from the commencement of the 1981 summer timetable and their eventual demise was completed in September 1983 following introduction of the Class 455 stock. This feature is a tribute to their sterling service and reliability over some three and a half decades.

Below:
On 23 August 1973 when this photograph was taken, the Class 4SUB units still numbered over 150 and were used extensively on local services to and from Waterloo, Victoria and London Bridge. Here No 4747 makes up the 10.14 Waterloo-Effingham Junction leaving Wimbledon.

Right:
An eight-car 4SUB formation with No 4607 leading leaves Clapham Junction on 4 June 1975 rostered for the 15.24 Waterloo-Guildford.

Below right:
4SUBs Nos 4641 and 4626 make up the 10.56 Shepperton-Waterloo, seen here coming off the slow line flyover at Wimbledon on a dull 9 March 1978. Ex-South Tyneside Class 2EPB No 5781 stands alongside Wimbledon depot.

4607
36

24

One of the spare driving motor brakes held at Old Oak Common HST Depot, No 43151, is decked out in BR's new style 'Executive' livery which is now being used on Victoria-Gatwick services as well as some HST sets. *British Rail*

InterCity 125
43151

Epsom
3
Gentlemen
4726
72

94
20

Left:
4SUB unit No 4726 arrives at Epsom on 25 March 1980 with the 14.44 Effingham Junction-Victoria service

Below left:
Making up the 15.57 Victoria-West Croydon service on 29 July 1981, two 4SUB units with No 4294 leading, thread Clapham Cutting after leaving Clapham Junction on their way towards the next stop — Wandsworth Common.

Right:
Passing an attractive setting near Earlsfield, 4SUBs Nos 4654 and 4668 head towards the terminus with the 17.14 Hampton Court-Waterloo.

Below:
A variety of electric units are on view inside Slade Green repair shops on 6 February 1982. Together with 4SUB No 4656 are, left to right, 2HAP No 6134 (now withdrawn), Class 416/1 2EPB No 5660 and Class 508 No 508.022. Works and shed scenes are made much easier to photograph when using a wide-angle lens such as the 24mm Nikkor optic that was fitted to record this scene.

Below:
The black and white photograph in this section shows the style of lettering applied to the coach sides of the 'Green SUB' No 4732. Colour is really necessary to do justice to the livery and this front end view of the unit shows the 'Southern' style lettering applied, albeit rather spoiled by the necessity of retaining the yellow face. The unit arrives at Epsom Downs station in September 1982 whilst operating the shuttle from Sutton. *Bill Walker*

Above right:
Another view of the 'Green SUB', this time being hauled by 1922 vintage London Transport electric locomotive No 12 *Sarah Siddons*. The pair had been on exhibition at Eastleigh Open Day in May 1983 and here pass New Malden on the journey from Eastleigh to Wimbledon. The compressors on the locomotive were unable to operate from the high voltage west of Pirbright Junction and were, therefore, isolated with the air supply being taken from the unit. *M. Pope*

Below right:
An unusual view of a 12-SUB formation passing Arundel station 'en route' to Selhurst as empty stock on 21 June 1983. *C. Burnham*

12
12
12

Arundel

4298
82

4714

Left:
Given a fresh paint job as late as May 1982, 4SUB No 4298 — in harness with sister unit No 4754 — heads through Clapham Cutting with a morning commuter service from Epsom to Victoria.

Below left:
The 15.19 Victoria-East Croydon train consisting of 'Marys' 4714 leading 4750, rolls into Wandsworth Common on 25 August 1982.

Right:
The livery applied to all the 4SUBs from new was Southern green with repainting to standard British Rail blue occurring from the late 1960s. In the autumn of 1982, four-car set No 4732 was the last of the class to be repainted and was outshopped from Selhurst Depot in original green with what was known as 'Sunshine' lettering on the driving ends and on each side of each car. Showing numbers 12354 and 12795 above the windows in Southern Railway style, No 4732 pulls away from Wandsworth Common on 25 August 1982 forming the 16.14 Victoria-Beckenham.

Below:
The modern overbridge that traverses the rebuilt London Bridge station contrasts with ageing 4SUB No 4719 on 13 September 1982 with the 16.47 London Bridge-Epsom.

In immaculate condition, 'Whistler' No 40.092 passes Golcar on the long climb to Standedge Tunnel on 12 October 1982 hauling train No 8M17, the 12.25 Monkton to Northwich freight. *C. K. Wilkinson*

The 09.05 Liverpool Lime Street to York train is photographed near Diggle about to enter Standedge Tunnel headed by Brush Class 47/4 No 47.458. Diggle yard used to be on the left of the picture.
Barrie Watkins

From the Exe to the Plym

Words and photographs by **Colin J. Marsden**

The 52 miles of main line between Exeter and Plymouth are probably the most famous tracks of the WR, if not of the entire BR network. The fame of this basically twin-tracked section is mainly attributable to the 12-mile section between Starcross and Newton Abbot which skirts the Exe estuary, passing along the world famous 'sea wall' between Dawlish and Teignmouth, and finally running parallel to the Teign estuary between Teignmouth and Newton Abbot, an area visited by thousands of holidaymakers each year, a vast number of whom are railway enthusiasts.

All rail traffic to and from Plymouth, and the Cornish towns beyond, has to traverse the steep gradients of the lush South Devon countryside between Exeter and Plymouth. One of the major 'hubs' of rail activity in Devon is Exeter St Davids, served by WR main line services, Northeast-Southwest inter-Regional trains, local services to and from Barnstaple and Exmouth, and not forgetting the regular London services via the old LSWR line to Waterloo. To the east of Exeter St Davids station lays a sizeable freight yard, which once generated a large quantity of traffic, but today it is more often used as a freight transfer recess point. Adjacent to the station is a small locomotive and carriage servicing point, where local DMUs are stabled when not in use, and Waterloo-Exeter loco-hauled formations are cleaned between journeys. The station area boasts two beautiful ex-GWR signalboxes. Exeter Middle and Exeter West, both scheduled for early replacement under the Exeter resignalling scheme already well under way.

Travelling west from Exeter the route passes through some of the poorer parts of the City towards Exeter St Thomas station, served only by infrequent local services to and from Paignton/ Plymouth. Carrying on from Exeter St Thomas the line soon reaches Exeter City Basin where the oil and bitumen freight terminals are situated, and then passes into the open countryside as it leaves the city boundaries. Exminster signalbox and freight loop lies just prior to the start of the line which follows the Exe estuary towards Starcross, where passengers may alight and catch the ferry to Exmouth. Onwards from Starcross the line passes through the picturesque countryside of Powderham Castle and estate, Cockwood Harbour and on to Dawlish Warren, where both an up and down passenger loop is provided. The station buildings here house a sizeable privately owned model railway and museum which is open to the public during the summer months. After leaving Dawlish Warren the line passes along the main sea wall section and heads for Dawlish, skirting the edge of the sea all the way.

Leaving Dawlish there are five short tunnels and the line continues to skirt the sea shore towards Teignmouth where it bears slightly inland before regaining the coastline to give spectacular views across the River Teign towards Shaldon. The coastal section continues until one mile east of Newton Abbot where it heads inland to visit the ancient Market Town. Sizeable freight yards once surrounded the station area but these have practically all closed, and the once thriving diesel depot and maintenance facilities have all gone. West of Newton Abbot there are four tracks for about one mile to Aller Junction where the Plymouth and Paignton lines divide. After negotiating the Aller pointwork the first of the Devon banks is encountered — Dainton, with a maximum climb of 1:36 near the summit at Dainton tunnel, from where the gradient drops steadily towards Totnes. To the east of Totnes station there is the terminus of the Dart Valley Light Railway line from Buckfastleigh. Totnes station has both up and down loop platform lines to cater for the passing of trains when the necessity arises. From Totnes station there is a steady climb towards Wrangaton passing through Tigley, Marley Tunnel and Brent on the way. Brent once housed a junction station for the Kingsbridge branch which closed for passengers from 16 September 1963; the main line station closed for traffic a year later. After Wrangaton the line drops downhill again through Ivybridge,

Above right:
Class 45 No 45.140 stands at Exeter St Davids with the 19.25 Penzance-Paddington 'up postal' on 14 July 1983; this train is normally operated by Classes 47 and 50.

Below right:
One of the most famous sights in Devon for a number of years has been the trains of 'tent top' clay wagons operating from the china clay quarries in Cornwall to various points throughout the country. Departing from Exeter with the City in the background, Class 47 No 47.205 hauls some empty wagons bound for Lostwithiel on 7 September 1983.

Cornwood and reaches the outskirts of the City of Plymouth at Plympton. Then follows Tavistock Junction where there is a freight yard, with the branch line to Marsh Mills diverging on the north side. The line then continues past Laira, the only diesel maintenance depot in Devon. Adjacent to the depot freight only lines diverge to Plymouth Friary and Plymstock freight terminals, which still generate two or three freight trains daily. The main line continues past Plymouth (Laira) Carriage Sidings and onwards to Plymouth North Road station.

Until the introduction of IC125 trains on Paddington services in the early 1980s, followed by Northeast-Southwest duties, passenger services were entirely worked by diesel-hauled trains and DMUs, with a wide variety of locomotive classes operating in the area. Today, apart from DMU and IC125 formations, operations are usually carried out by Classes 08, 31, 33, 37, 45, 46, 47 and 50, with the likelihood of an ever increasing number of Class 56 visitors as crews become trained on them. Passenger flow on the main line during weekdays is approximately two trains per hour in each direction with the occasional freight train as required. On summer Saturdays passenger traffic increases drastically with an endless array of loco-hauled trains from all parts of the country convering on the West Country, giving the enthusiast a vast number of trains to observe or photograph. The following illustrations give an example of the scenes to be observed in South Devon.

Above:
An unexpected arrival at Exeter St Davids on 17 June 1983 was Electroputere Class 56 No 56.047 hauling Class 50 No 50.031 *Hood* on the 14.45 Paddington-Plymouth. The 'Hoover' had failed near Westbury and the freight locomotive was given a break from normal stone train haulage in order to assist.
Charles E. Beatson

Below:
On a beautiful August day in 1981, Brush Class 47/4 No 47.510 *Fair Rosamund* notches up leaving Exeter St Davids with the 07.40 Penzance-Liverpool Lime Street. *J. F. Medley*

62

Left:
From the introduction of the summer timetable in May 1983, the local services from Exeter to Paignton have been diagrammed for Class 33 operation. No 33.058 approaches Exminster on 7 September 1983 with the 09.25 Exeter-Paignton local service.

Below left:
With I. K. Brunel's Atmospheric Railway building in the background, Class 31 No 31.294 passes through the platforms at Starcross with empty vans from Plymouth to Old Oak Common on 29 June 1981.

Right:
Skirting the sea wall between Dawlish and Dawlish Warren is Class 25 No 25.058 with a Paignton-Exeter summer local on 19 June 1980. The Class 25s were eliminated from Devon operations during 1980/81 in favour of Classes 31 and 33.

Below:
With the scenic South Devon countryside as a backdrop Class 50 No 50.011 *Centurion* passes Bishopsteignton between Teignmouth and Newton Abbot, with the 07.20 Penzance-Liverpool on 6 September 1983.

Brush Class 31 No 31.239 pilots Class 50 No 50.041 *Bulwark* on a westbound goods train climbing Rattery Bank on 19 July 1982. *Bulwark* was the locomotive involved in the Paddington derailment on 23 November 1983 and is now in course of extensive repairs.
Brian Stephenson

Above:
Semaphore signalling still prevails in the Newton Abbot area but with MAS schemes well under way, colour light equipment will soon be erected. Departing from Newton Abbot and passing the West signalbox, Class 31 No 31.410 hauls special ECS from Exeter to Plymouth on 17 September 1982.

Below:
Nearing the top of the climb at Dainton bank and heading towards the tunnel, Class 47 No 47.188 hauls a Severn Tunnel Junction-Plymouth air-braked freight on 12 September 1983.

Left:
Approaching Totnes from the west Class 50 No 50.043 *Eagle* takes the platform line loop with the 16.30 Plymouth-Paddington Sunday service on 14 September 1983.

Below left:
On the outskirts of Plymouth, between Tavistock Junction and Laira Junction, IC125 set No 253.038 hurries towards Plymouth with the 08.25 Paddington-Penzance on 15 September 1982. The lines in the foreground are the entrance/exit to part of Laira depot and the Plymouth Friary freight line.

Above:
Passing Laira carriage washing machine Class 45 No 45.041 *Royal Tank Regiment* hauls the 03.45 Severn Tunnel Junction-Plymouth Friary freight on the final leg of its journey on 15 September 1982.

Below:
The early morning sun glints on IC125 No 253.010 as it approaches Langstone Rock, near Dawlish Warren, with empty stock from Plymouth to Exeter on 22 June 1981. The town of Dawlish can be seen in the background.

Crossing the Pennines via Diggle

Words and photographs by **John Vaughan**

Although business travels have frequently taken me from my home on the Sussex coast to the Northern Counties, and travels over the years have resulted in the traversal of most northern rail routes, it was not until the summer of 1983 that an invitation from old friend and fellow railway photographer Gavin Morrison resulted in me spending a few days 'line-siding' on the cross-Pennine 'Diggle' route. I vividly recalled seeing photographs in issues of *Trains Illustrated* in the mid-1950s showing the deep industrial valleys of the West Riding of Yorkshire with the plethora of textile mills and associated tall dark chimneys but what could be expected in these days of rationalisation and InterCity travel was an unknown quantity.

Not surprisingly the general topography has not changed and the scenery on both sides of the Pennines is magnificent. However many of the fine old mills and their aesthetically pleasing chimneys have disappeared as the far more functional buildings of the present century take over and modern industrial estates expand. While many of the long rows of terraced houses survive there are also piles of rubble where others have been demolished, vacated by mill workers after they were forced to move away in the wake of mechanisation and the large scale importation of

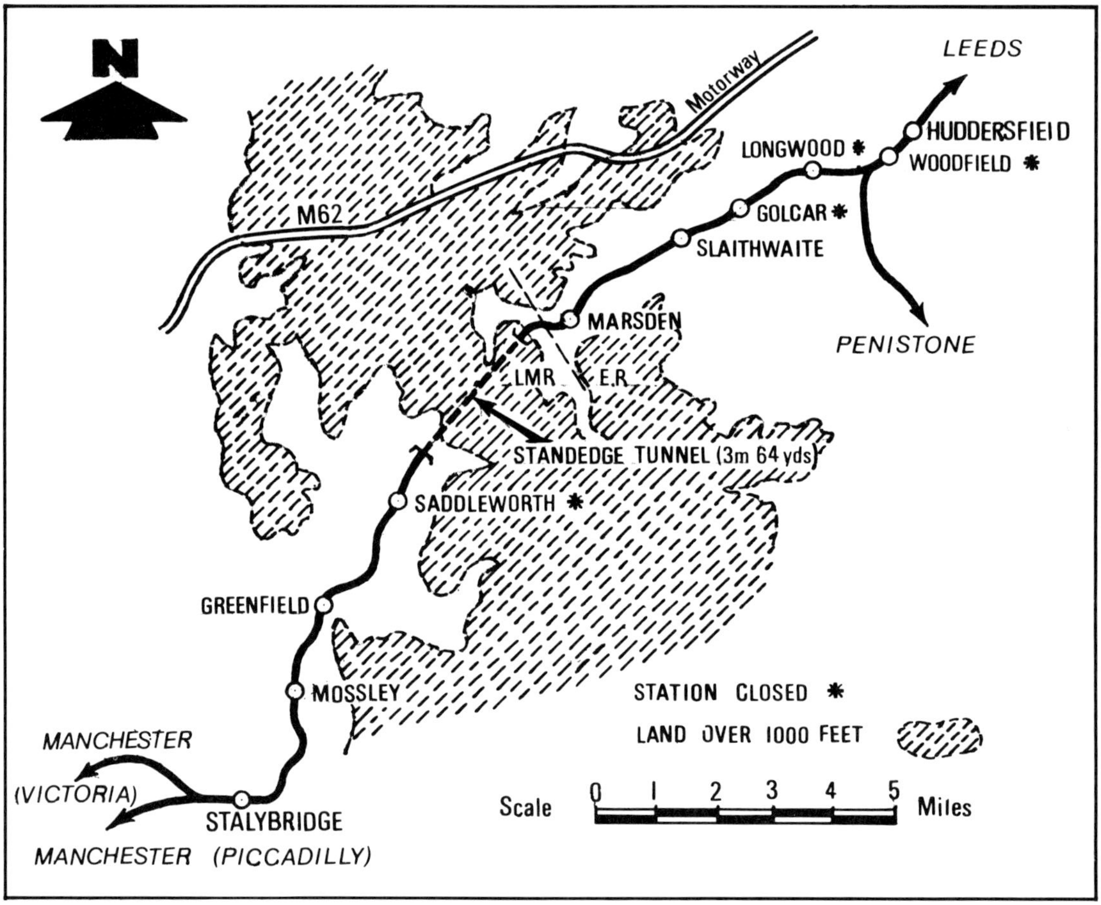

Below:
The summit of the 18-mile former LNWR route between Stalybridge and Huddersfield is the 3 mile 64yd long Standedge tunnel. With the closure of the GCR Woodhead route and the reduction to secondary status of the L&YR Calder Valley, line, the Diggle route and the Hope Valley line are now the main cross-Pennine arteries between Greater Manchester and the Yorkshire centres of Leeds and Sheffield. Emerging from Standedge on 16 June 1983 and passing Marsden's distant signal is No 45.074 with the 11.15 Bangor-Scarborough. Note the old disused bore on the left.

products from the Far East. With the increase in the use of oil, gas and electricity by householders and industry alike and with the abolition of the steam engine and the introduction of legislation controlling pollution, the Pennine air is clear and free from the smog usually associated with the burning of coal.

As regards the railway, there have obviously been changes over recent years and, in common with most other areas, the general theme is one of rationalisation. While one or two passing loops survive, the main line has been reduced from four to two tracks and most sidings have been removed. It is now only the older generation who can remember railway curiosities such as the Deiph branch which closed in the mid-1950s. In parts the 18 route miles from Stalybridge to Huddersfield have seen little investment, although most of the main line does comprise flat bottomed continuously welded rail and Slaithwaite station was reopened during 1982. On the other hand manual signalling survives — it is quite adequate as the speed restricted route provides few opportunities for high speed rail travel.

Since the closure of the Woodhead route additional traffic has been diverted over the ex-London & North Western Railway 'Diggle' line and the ex-Midland Railway's Hope Valley route but any enthusiast who thinks that these main arteries are going to produce an endless procession of rumbling freight trains is going to be disappointed. Traffic of this type is very erratic and a couple of hours can pass without a single freight traversing the Pennines in either direction. Most of what does appear comprises HAA merry-go-round hoppers plying to and from Fiddlers Ferry. Other than the handful of local diesel multiple-units, all trains over Diggle are locomotive-hauled and the InterCity 125 unit has yet to arrive. The service on the main line is hourly in each direction with additional workings at peak times and during the height of the summer.

The passenger trains are hauled by Class 45/1 or 47/4 locomotives, although in summer variety can be increased by the appearance of subdivisions of the classes, especially Classes 45/0 and 47/0. On a good day during the 1983 summer Class 40 and 46 locomotives also appeared. Class 56s are gradually taking over from the Class 47/3s on the merry-go-round workings and other freight can produce Classes 31, 37, 40 and 45. With major depots such as Healey Mills and Longsight on either side of the Pennines the class of motive power is never entirely predictable which can prove to be a source of excitement for the railway photographer. Occasionally freight trains are held in the loops on either side of Standedge tunnel and it doesn't pay to change location immediately a passenger service has passed as quite often a freight will follow within a few minutes. However the freight scene has changed with the times and the MGR workings, with their modern wagons and braking systems, can travel at passenger train speeds over much of the route and the empty MGRs rarely find themselves 'looped'.

The vantage points for the railway photographer are numerous. Obviously it helps to be in the company of one of the northern experts but with a choice of supplementary lenses it is

possible to get really attractive photographs at most locations. It is, of course, a challenge to produce a portfolio of prints which convey the atmosphere of the countryside and of the trains running through it. I would not claim for one minute that I have been successful in this after only a single visit but certainly this one trip was enough to whet the appetite and make me look forward to another lineside sortie. All of the photographs illustrated in this feature were taken with a Pentax 6×7 camera using 105mm, 200mm and 300mm lenses except for the Class 40 which was captured by a 35mm Nikon FM2 camera fitted with a 85mm f2 Nikkor lens. My thanks go to Gavin Morrison for his assistance in the selection of vantage points.

Left:
When the Woodhead route was closed in July 1981 the substantial merry-go-round traffic between the Yorkshire coalfields and Fiddlers Ferry, near Widnes, was diverted to the Diggle route and Class 56 locomotives were drafted into the area to haul the trains. Descending through Paddock near Huddersfield on 15 June 1983 is No 56.022 with eastbound empties. The number of mills and chimneys in the West Riding is forever dwindling but a fine example can be seen to the left of the viaduct.

Above:
On weekdays there is an hourly main line train in each direction linking Liverpool and North Wales with Scarborough and Newcastle; additional local trains run at irregular intervals. Freight traffic is very erratic but a handful of trains cross the Pennines during the daylight hours. Thrashing up the bank and through the cutting at Paddock, just west of Huddersfield, is No 37.036 with a long coal haul. The track has been reduced from four to two lines, or 'dequadrified' in today's jargon.

Above:
A sight and sound to warm the hearts of the Class 40 fans. Class 40 workings at the head of passenger trains in the summer of 1983 were very unpredictable but on Saturday 18 June 1983 No 40.141 was rostered on the 08.40SO Manchester-Scarborough and the 12.00SO return. Attacking the Pennines at Longwood with its returning seven-coach load is the venerable 22-year old split headcode panel locomotive with, seemingly, a generous sprinkling of bellowers in the leading coach.

Below:
The Diggle route climbs through Golcar, Linthwaite, Slaithwaite and Marsden to cross the Eastern Region/ Midland Region boundary just east of Standedge tunnel. Passing the boundary with the 14.05 Liverpool-Newcastle is Class 45/1 'Peak' No 45.149. The load includes Mark 2a, 2b and 2d coaches. In the background is the splendid Pennine scenery and in the left foreground is a passing loop for slow moving freights. Sadly these passenger services cannot compete in time with road transport using the cross-Pennine M62 Motorway.

Above:
While the Class 45 'Peak' varieties are no strangers to the Diggle route, since their replacement from the Midland main line they have become far more common and now numerically share services with the evergreen Class 47s. With the western portal on Standedge tunnel just visible under the distant road bridge No 47.528 passes Diggle Junction with the 14.50 York-Liverpool. Diggle station closed in October 1968 but perhaps surprisingly, semaphore signalling survives.

Below:
A view looking westward from Diggle towards Saddleworth. The only remarkable thing about the photograph is that both up and down main line trains can be seen. Disappearing towards Manchester is No 45.135 with the 15.00 Scarborough-Liverpool while heading towards the camera is No 47.426 with the 15.05 Bangor-Scarborough. Just above the Class 47 is a tunnel which once carried the tracks of the long-closed Friezland Loop line, which was an alternative route from Diggle to Stalybridge.

Below:
The substantial scale of the surroundings dwarf 136-ton 'Peak' No 45.145 which is framed by three fine rhododendron shrubs as it descends from Midge Hill and through Mossley with the 16.00 Scarborough-Liverpool. The majority of trains over the Diggle route are locomotive-hauled, the scenery is splendid and a visit for the railway photographer can be highly recommended.

The Human Interest

All photographs by **Brian Morrison** unless otherwise indicated

Railways are run by people for people. Yet many photographers try to avoid the inclusion of the human element in their work. Where they meet one of the loonies who jumps out in front of a photographer just as the train arrives or where it is one of the waving arms protruding from the carriages of a special working, their objection is very understandable. When it is a railwayman or passengers, however, in a natural environment, to include the human interest can turn a mundane picture into an interesting one.

Above:
Two local youths are used as props to lead the eye to the train which, otherwise, could be lost amid the surrounding mass of Medway town dwellings. On 29 May 1981 two Class 414/3 2HAP EMUs with No 6159 leading, form the 15.35 Charing Cross to Gillingham via Erith and cross the Luton Arches between Chatham and Gillingham.

Above:
Well wrapped up against the elements, the passengers that have alighted at Millom from the 14.20 Carlisle-Preston DMU on 10 February 1983 lend to the scene the appearance of a Lowry painting.

Top right:
On a warm September evening in 1982, the passengers for the 18.12 to Reigate at London Bridge contrast well with the previous scene. Light summer jackets, shirts and blouses predominate as they board Class 423/0 4VEP EMU No 7873.

Bottom right:
The opportunity to 'cab' a 'Deltic' produces a scene of animation at Newcastle on an August day in 1978 as the local youngsters all climb aboard for a fleeting visit. No 55.006 *The Fife and Forfar Yeomanry* heads the 09.00 Aberdeen-King's Cross.

13

31124

Left:
A Class 117 Pressed Steel Company DMU makes a smokey exit away from Southall on 20 March 1976 watched by one of the number of Pakistani police officers who have been appointed in the area to administer British law and order to the large community of Asians

Below:
Early morning at Rugby on 29 October 1983. Class 31/1 No 31.124 stands in the south end bay while a lone railwayman strolls down the platform to his place of work. *Geoff Dowling*

Above:
The driver of a Waterloo & City Class 487 EMU awaits the 'right away' at Waterloo on 28 September 1982 before taking his charge rumbling through the tunnel on the five-minute journey to Bank station.

Above:
Passengers for the 14.25 departure for Airdrie walk down the Milngavie platform on 26 January 1981 seeking a suitable seat for their journey in Class 303 EMU No 303.036.

Top right:
A particularly mixed bag of passengers watch the arrival of their train at Ponders End. Class 305/1 EMU No 423 forms the 11.40 Hertford East-Liverpool Street on a chilly February morning in 1976.

Bottom right:
In typical pose, the station officer at Spondon dares the passenger to open his door before the train has come to a halt! On 27 June 1983 the 14.34 Lincoln-Crewe service comprises BR Swindon Class 120 cars Nos M53715/59264/53687.

2P59
423

Above:
Early on a May morning in 1980 the 07.15 Edinburgh-King's Cross HST set is making the scheduled stop at Berwick-upon-Tweed. A late rising passenger runs frantically towards the station to board before it is too late.

Above:
Class 411/2 4CEP EMU No 7190 (since refurbished and renumbered 1568) forms the 13.28 Ramsgate-Charing Cross service on 26 May 1981. Its progress through Folkestone Warren is watched by two teenagers.

0000

Left:
Storm clouds threaten as Class 47/4 No 47.427 rolls the up 'Clansman' for Euston into Aviemore on 28 May 1976. Holidaymakers returning home make up the majority of the passengers.

Below left:
Raincoats and plastic scarves are the order of the day for the passengers as the arrival of the 09.00 Sunday service from Edinburgh to Inverness coincides with the rain letting up for a time over Pitlochry. Class 25/2 No 25.228 pilots Class 26/1 No 26.034 on 29 May 1977.

Below:
On a sweltering 26 August 1981, passengers from the 14.42 Sittingbourne-Sheerness trudge down the Queenborough platform towards the exit. The train consists of Class 414/3 2HAP EMUs Nos 6112 and 6086.

Above:
One man and his dog. A scene on the Erewash Valley Line at Stanton in June 1983.

Right:
With the third-rail current switched off, track repairs are carried out near Mottingham following a derailment on 11 October 1977.

From a Different Point of View

Basically railway photographs are a record of what was before the camera lens at the time. Photographers usually strive to obtain good detail in the subject matter and also to include something of the environs to indicate to the viewer where the scene was taken. This is all to the good and the well taken, sharp, front 'three-quarters' view of a train in the landscape will always predominate in published railway photographs.

Sometimes it is refreshing to depart from accepted tradition, however, and to try to produce a thought out railway picture as opposed to a usual type of railway photograph. There are no set rules and the results can be as diverse as the cameraman's 'seeing eye' or imagination. Sometimes quite mundane views can be enlivened by taking photographs through available 'props' such as trees, gates and the like or by including something of the foreground interest with use of a short focus wide-angle lens or by compressing and exaggerating the background with a long focus telephoto.

On the premise that one picture is worth a thousand words perhaps the following selection will stimulate the reader to keep an eye open for that elusive masterpiece?

Below:
A very clever and perfectly executed photograph through a wide angle lens of Class 56 No 56.087 stabled at Landore Freightliner Terminal on 10 September 1983. A 'straight' view of 56.087 would have resulted in a locomotive portrait; by taking it through a car windscreen after heavy rain the result is much enhanced. *Geoff Dowling*

Right:
Backlighting has ensured that the spray from the Penzance Ponsondane carriage washer is shown up to maximum effect as High Speed Train set No 253.004 receives a welcome shower after working into the Cornish terminus on a hot 3 July 1982 with the 'Cornish Riviera' from Paddington. The scene was recorded on a Nikon 35mm camera fitted with a 105mm medium telephoto lens. *Brian Morrison*

Above:
Shortly after passing Ferryhill depot and Craighinches yard, the line to the south from Aberdeen leaves behind the last of the City's suburbs and after passing Nigg Bay and Cove Bay, hugs the North Sea coastline. Approaching the sea at Nigg Bay Brush Class 47/4 No 47.412 notches up with the 12.35 Aberdeen-Edinburgh. A 300mm telephoto lens on a Bronica camera was used to bring out the background for maximum effect. *Brian Morrison*

Below:
Taken from almost the same position as the previous scene, on this occasion a wide angle lens has produced a completely different perspective. Another Brush '47/4' No 47.540 provides the power. *Brian Morrison*

Above:
On 11 May 1983, Class 121 Pressed Steel Co single unit No W55025 runs alongside the East Looe river, between Looe and Sandplace, with the 10.05 Looe-Liskeard, accelerating away from the severe permanent way slack of an ungated level crossing. It would have been easy to have recorded this unit from trackside but by moving back and including the fencing, the river, the steam age level crossing sign and the raised footway — essential at high tide when the road is submerged — the photographer has produced an excellent railway picture. *John Whitehouse*

Left:
The 14.38 Paignton-Liverpool Lime Street is caught through some lineside branches near Standish on 8 May 1982 headed by Class 45/0 No 45.014. On a dull day a standard 50mm lens was used on a Nikon 35mm camera with an exposure of 1/500th at f4.
Brian Morrison

Left:
Two views through parts of station buildings where the train is only a small object in the overall scene but is, nevertheless, positioned in such a way that the eye goes directly to it. (Top) Class 415/1 4EPB EMU No 5154 draws into Eltham Park station in southeast London as the 13.04 Dartford-Cannon Street. The graffiti covering the station approach will not be removed by station staff in the usual way because the station is due to close as soon as the new Eltham station is completed.

Below left:
One clean pane of glass in an otherwise dirt-encrusted window is used to good effect to frame a fast moving High Speed Train charging through a rain-swept Bridgwater on 23 September 1982. Note how the headlight of the power car is reflected on the wet platform. *Both: Brian Morrison*

Below:
A well planned picture of a 'Hoover' and its reflection. In soft early spring lighting Class 50 No 50.032 *Courageous* heads south on 24 March 1982 with the 10.23 Manchester Piccadilly-Plymouth alongside the Worcester Canal at Birmingham University.
Geoff Dowling

Above:
A real 'train in the landscape' picture. On a blustery September day in 1983, a Class 118 BRCW suburban three-car DMU seems to be perched atop the cliff overlooking Carbis Bay in Cornwall as it works the St Erth-St Ives service. *John Whitehouse*

Below:
Caught nicely between the signalbox and a part of the station building. Class 40 No 40.056 passes through Helsby Junction on 18 September 1981 with westbound tanks from Warrington bound for Stanlow on the Helsby-Hooton line. *Brian Morrison*

Right:
Framed in the opening to the goods shed at Dingwall, the driver of Class 26/1 No 26.031 prepares to hand the 'tablet' to the waiting signalman before proceeding into the station with the 17.45 Inverness-Kyle of Lochalsh on 30 May 1977. *Brian Morrison*

Northwards from Aberdeen

Words and photographs by **Brian Morrison**

There was a time when lines northward from Aberdeen radiated to Fraserburgh, Peterhead, Old Meldrum, Alford, Boddam and Macduff in addition to the Great North of Scotland Railway route to Inverness via both Portsoy and Keith. Today only the Inverness line via Keith remains with the myriad stations en route being reduced to embrace only the few major townships such as Inverurie, Insch, Huntly, Keith etc.

The service from the Granite City to the Highland capital is not of the best but is adequate, with some seven trains a day running at two-hourly intervals. Except for a Sunday service that travels from Glasgow to Inverness via Aberdeen, it is necessary to change at Aberdeen for the remaining journey northwards and it is usual for your train to be entrusted to a Class 26 or 27 although Class 47s, 40s and 25s are not unknown. All this is a vast improvement on the diesel multiple-units that were used for the journey of over 100 miles for a number of years before locomotive-hauled stock took over.

Freight is now minimal; the fish traffic now comes in to Aberdeen by road from Fraserburgh and Peterhead, and other non-passenger workings are restricted to the occasional trip working with special interest being focused on the well known whisky train.

The illustrations show the character of the line at the eastern extremity from Aberdeen to Keith — a much under-photographed stretch.

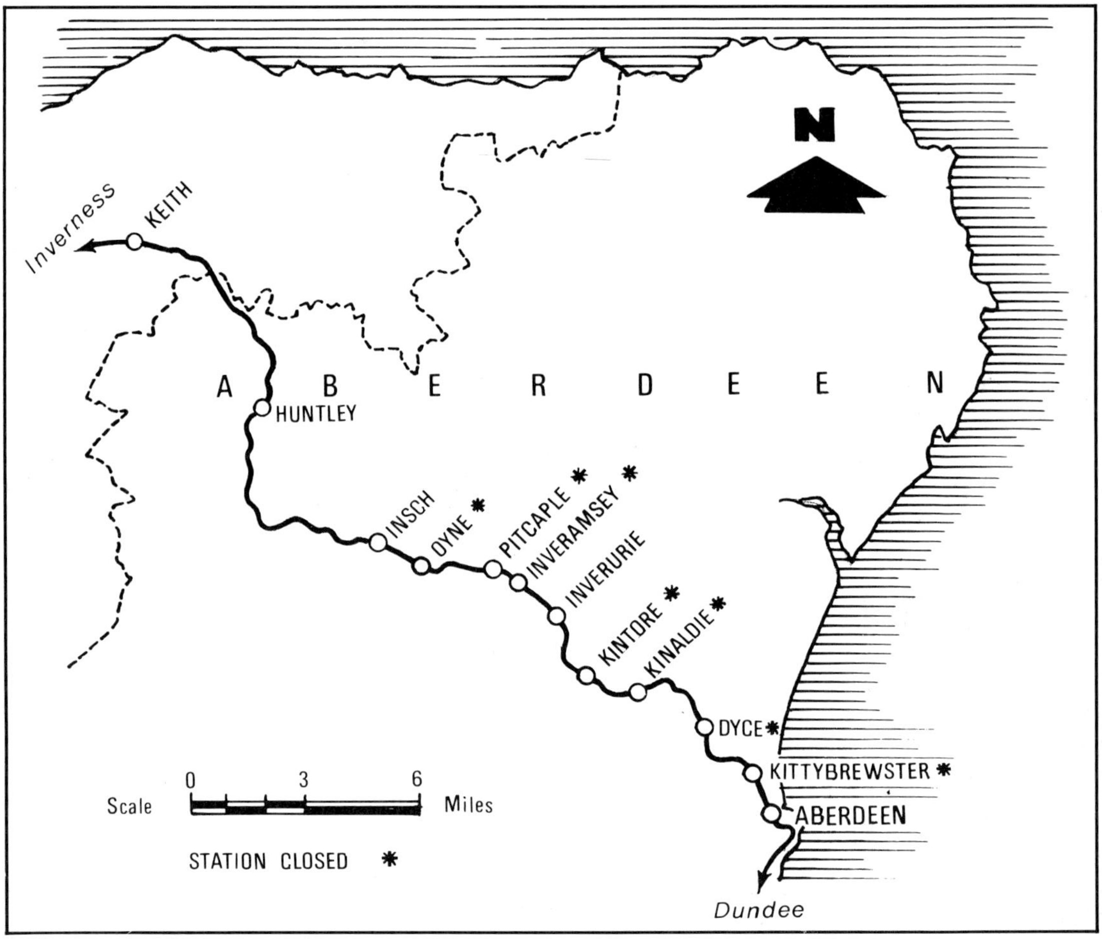

Above:
Train services northwards from Aberdeen now only have need of one platform and the once extensive expanse of the old Aberdeen Joint station is the subject of redevelopment. With demolition and building work going on all around, Class 27/1 No 27.109 waits for the clock hands to reach 11.52 before setting off for Inverness on 20 April 1982.

Below:
Rolling into Aberdeen from the north, the unusually routed Sunday only 16.25 Inverness to Glasgow Queen Street via Aberdeen is in the charge of Brush Class 47/4 No 47.519 on 18 April 1982.

Above left:
Passing the site of the old Schoolhill station that was closed 45 years before, the 15.47 Aberdeen-Inverness prepares to enter the short tunnel that will take the train on to the climb to Kittybrewster. Class 26/1 No 26.036 provides the motive power.

Below left:
Climbing away from Aberdeen towards Kittybrewster, Class 26/1 No 26.033 hauls the 15.47 to Inverness where arrival is timed for 18.23.

Above:
With the old platform of closed Kittybrewster just visible through the road bridge, Class 08 No 3677 (later renumbered 08.515) struggles up the 1 in 72 incline with a load for the coal depot at Kittybrewster on 27 March 1974.

Below:
A reminder of the days when the Class 24s were a part of the British Rail fleet. With an unlikely looking mixed load en route from Inverurie to Ferryhill, Class 24/2 No 24.070 passes Dyce Junction on 25 March 1974.

Above:
Chivas Regal whisky containers from Elgin are taken through the remains of Dyce Junction on 20 April 1982 by Class 25/1 No 25.079 and head towards Aberdeen.

Below:
Passengers no more: all that remains of the once important Dyce Junction. On the far left a train heads for Inverness past the desolation in the foreground, once the platforms for the Fraserburgh and Peterhead lines. The front of the wooden building on the right is currently a DIY shop.

Above:
Although photographed as recently as April 1982, these remains of Kinaldie station buildings have now been razed and only the grass-covered platforms remain. In the distance Class 26/0 No 26.014 approaches with the 14.43hr Inverness-Aberdeen train.

Below:
Still clearly displaying the name Oyne, only the grassy platform shows that this station is no longer in service; in fact, it was closed to passengers in May 1968. (Photographed on 17 April 1982.)

Above:
Passing the point north of Kintore where the Alford branch once diverged, No 26.033 heads the six Mk 1 bogies that make up the 10.38 Inverness-Aberdeen on 22 April 1982. The Alford line closed to passengers in January 1950 and Kintore station in December 1964.

Left:
Contrasts at Inverurie. On 20 April 1982 Class 27/1 No 27.107 prepares to make the scheduled stop with the 09.44 Aberdeen-Inverness. As can be seen from the 1973 photograph of a Swindon Class 120 dmu on a similar service, the platform awnings of the station have gone and no station buildings remain on the up side. Otherwise Inverurie station appears in good condition!

Top right:
Passing through a section of Scottish countryside that used to be part of the Pitcaple Castle estate, No 27.109 heads towards Inveramsey with the 08.26 from Inverness. At Inveramsey the lengthy branch to Macduff diverged until its closure in October 1951.

Bottom right:
Hammering through the wide open countryside near Insch, Class 47/0 No 47.160 has been rostered for the 11.52 Aberdeen-Inverness and has no problems with just six bogies.

Above:
Running alongside the River Bogie at Braeside of Cults, between Huntly and Insch, No 27.107 again is rostered for the 14.43 Inverness-Aberdeen.

Left:
On 17 April 1982 the 13.53 Aberdeen-Inverness train arrives at Huntly hauled by 27.109. All the Class 27/1 subdivision were locomotives fitted for 'push and pull' working when the Glasgow-Edinburgh services utilised a locomotive at each end of the stock. Now operated by Class 47/7s, the '27/1s' were released; they have since had the 'push and pull' apparatus removed and have all been renumbered into the '27/0' series. This locomotive now carries the number 27.053; No 27.107 (photograph above) is now 27.051.

Below:
Leaving the township of Keith behind, the 12.43 Inverness-Aberdeen makes for the next stop of Huntly on a cloudless April afternoon in 1982 headed by Class 47/0 No 47.141 of the Glasgow Eastfield allocation.

Frame Two!

Photographs by **Brian Morrison**

On busy stretches of line the opportunity sometimes occurs for two moving trains to be included in the one photograph. Good timing, the correct length lens and a not inconsiderable slice of luck are the main ingredients of the following scenes.

Below:
As Class 416/1 2EPB EMU No 5660 leaves Denmark Hill station in southeast London on 9 August 1982 with the 14.49 Battersea Park-London Bridge, a Class 73/1 electro-diesel hauling coal hoppers silently glides into the picture heading towards Nunhead with a Stewarts Lane to Hoo Junction train travelling via the Dartford Loop. The large building in the background is the famous King's College Hospital.

Above:
Class 86/0 No E3153 (now No 86.039) races past Brent yards on the approach to Wembley Central on 26 June 1973 with a Euston-Blackpool express in tow. Pulling away from the yards on the left following a locomotive change is the 14.00 Dagenham-Garston 'Silcock & Collins Group' cartic with Class 81 No E3096 (now No 81.021) at the working end.

Below:
A piquant contrast between Waterloo and Vauxhall on 5 April 1982. With a background of old and new buildings a new Class 508 EMU forms a local service to Kingston and runs alongside one of the now withdrawn Class 405/2 4SUBs working a Waterloo-Wimbledon-Richmond-Waterloo roundabout service. Unit numbers are 508.020 and 4658.

Above right:
It is rare indeed for two oncoming freights to appear at the same time but this is just what transpired at Normanton-on-Soar, near Loughborough, on 28 June 1983. On the left Class 45/0 'Peak' No 45.004 *Royal Irish Fusilier* hauls a rake of fitted coal hoppers and overtakes Class 20s Nos 20.163 and 20.193 with a ballast train.

Below right:
A busy scene at Pengam, near Cardiff, on 9 June 1982. Class 25s Nos 25.313 and 25.072 head a down Freightliner round the loop to Long Dyke Junction during a shunting manoeuvre as Class 37 No 37.254 passes in the opposite direction with an up coal train.

37254

Above:
As a BR Derby Class 108 twin unit consisting of driving trailer composite No M56213 and driving motor brake second No M50625 takes the old Cheshire Lines route to Manchester with the 10.28 Chester-Manchester Oxford Road, a Class 40 No 40.188 'whistles' around the curve and into Chester from the opposite direction hauling the late running 09.30 Crewe-Holyhead on 19 September 1981.

Below:
A well timed 'catch' at the junction of the Sinfin branch near Peartree, Derby on 1 July 1983. An unidentified Class 254 HST forming the 06.46 Newcastle-Plymouth, passes a BR Swindon Class 120 Cross-Country three-car DMU that makes up the 07.30 Lincoln-Birmingham New Street.

Above right:
A very low late evening sun on 1 June 1981 casts its final rays on a pair of Class 37s heading up and down Cambridge trains between Newport and Elsenham. Heading towards the camera No 37.090 powers the 18.22 Liverpool Street departure and making rapid strides southwards is 37.097 with the 18.50 ex-Cambridge.

Below right:
A stroke of good fortune at the west end of Clapham Junction on 1 October 1983 as a new Class 455 EMU No 5830 heads towards the Capital forming a local for Waterloo at the same time as the 13.10 Waterloo-Exeter St Davids roars through the station behind 'Hoover' No 50.047 *Swiftsure*.

5830

The Line to Rhymney

Photographs by **Brian Morrison**

Visitors seeking a great variety of motive power will not be rewarded by a trip from Cardiff, north to the small town of Rhymney (or Rhymni to give it the correct Welsh spelling) but those looking for a line of character and individuality and steeped in the history of the Welsh Valley will not be in the least disappointed. Basically the local service is in the hands of either Derby Class 116 or Pressed Steel Company Class 117 diesel multiple-units and the freight is monopolised by the Class 37 work horses.

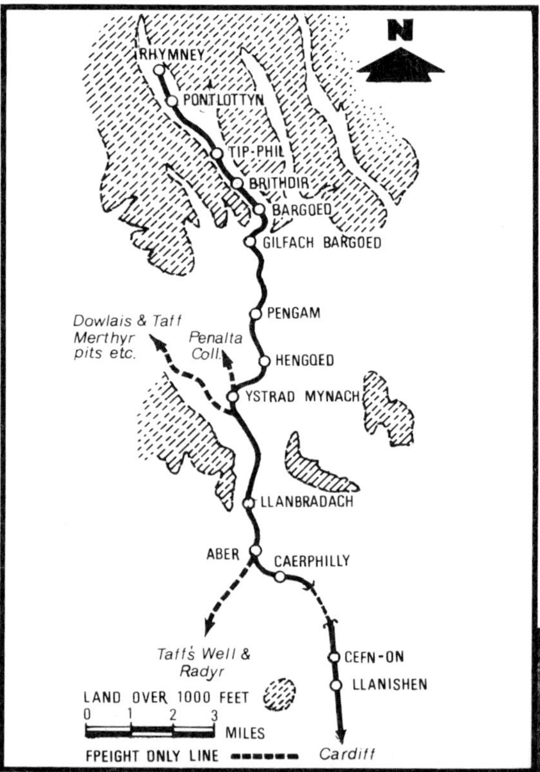

Below:
With a merry-go-round coal train for Aberthaw Power Station, Class 37s Nos 37.297 and 37.394 hammer through Llanishen station while the morning DMU from Penarth to Rhymney exchanges a few passengers on the down platform.

Above:
With the buildings that once housed the Rhymney Railway's Caerphilly Works on the right, more MGR coal for Aberthaw is on the way, hauled on this occasion by Nos 37.281 and 37.295. Note Canton's new style front end numbering, now to be seen on a number of the locomotives allocated to the Cardiff depot.

Below:
Merry-go-round empties from Aberthaw are powered through Llanbradach on 11 June 1982 by Nos 37.294 and 37.297.

Top:
On the same day another return empty MGR working snakes through Ystrad Mynach to obtain a refill at Penalta Colliery, the line for which can be seen branching off to the left just in front of the leading Class 37.

Above:
Photographed between Hengoed and Ystrad Mynach, the 14.20 Rhymney to Penarth local service is formed of the usual BR Derby Class 116 three-car surburban DMU, with driving motor brake second class car No W50088 leading.

Above:
In short-lived white livery with blue body stripe, another Class 116 unit — here forming the 11.28 Rhymney-Penarth — draws to a stand at the neat little station of Bargoed on 15 September 1979.

Below:
At Brithdir platform (one can hardly call it a station) a Pressed Steel Co Class 117 DMU provides a change from the normal Class 116 restarting the 16.28 Rhymney-Cardiff Bute Road from the obligatory stop on 11 June 1982. The prefix 'C' on the front number indicates that the unit is allocated to Cardiff Division.

Bottom:
The terminus of Rhymney in June 1982 with another Class 117 unit waiting for the time to return to the Welsh capital following arrival as the 13.53 from Penarth. Unit No C450 is led by driving motor brake second No W51352.

35mm Rules OK?

The case for the smaller camera

Words and photographs by **Brian Morrison**

It must appear rather strange for someone who has used large format cameras for over 30 years to start expounding on the virtues of the 35mm variety, but the fact is I have been converted.

The term 'large format', of course, is relative. When I commenced railway photography in the early 1950s my $2\frac{1}{4}$in $\times$ $2\frac{1}{4}$in Agfa Isolette was certainly not considered as a large camera, with the likes of Maurice Earley, Eric Treacy, Frank Hebron, Ernest Wethersett and many others all toting quarter-plate reflexes, or even larger, about the lineside. I even tried an old pre-World War 2 Thornton Pickard quarter-plate myself for a time and, when it decided to function properly, it produced some of my best results of the period. However I remained faithful to the $2\frac{1}{4}$in square format through the years with two Isolettes, a Rollieflex and a number of Bronicas.

A few years ago I obtained a 35mm Nikon camera on which to take colour transparencies alongside the large format black and white and I had both cameras with me when embarking on a two-week holiday in Cornwall. The shutter on the new Bronica jammed solid on the first day! Not relishing the prospect of a return trip to Kent to fetch the older and more reliable Bronica I decided to try the then new Ilford XP1 film in the Nikon for the duration of the holiday and to forsake colour. Prints up to 10in $\times$ 8in from the developed negatives were good enough for the difference between them and similar size enlargements from large format Kodak Tri-X at the same speed rating of 400ASA to be hardly noticeable. In fact I was quite delighted with the results but was still loath to discard the Bronica and its accompanying lenses and I carried both cameras around for over a year.

Eventually I came to the conclusion that the larger and very much heavier equipment had no significant advantages over the lightweight Nikon and disposed of everything. The lesser burden, the ease and speed of operation of the small camera coupled with the much lower cost per negative, the multiplicity of lenses and the light imput allowed by lenses as large as f1.4 has brought about a new feeling in me, rather akin to shedding the heavy, uncomfortable clothes of winter for the pleasant lightweight apparel of spring and summer. I find I can continue to take photographs for quite some time after my colleagues with the large cameras have had to give up, as their f2.8 lenses do not allow the same light imput as mine, and they also have problems with depth of focus on the large cameras which is almost inconsequential with 35mm users.

And, at long last, my slightly drooping left shoulder is beginning to raise itself to the level of the other one again!

Left:
The exposure indicated at Lymington Pier station on a very foggy November afternoon was $\frac{1}{30}$th at f2.8. Had I been using a large format camera I would have needed a tripod and an exposure of $\frac{1}{4}$sec at f8 in order to obtain the same effect.

Above:
Both elbows on the wall, a small jump, camera to the upright position, an almost imperciptable click and this photograph is the result. Note particularly the depth of focus allowed by the Nikon FM2's standard 50mm lens in taking this scene at Skipton. A variety of motive power is shown: stabled Class 25/2s Nos 25.229 and 25.138 in the foreground; No 31.118 with a coal train in the background; a Class 108 DMU in the platform with the 09.19 Morecambe-Leeds service; and another unit of the same type in the siding.

Above:
When the first Southern Region Class 455 EMU was put on show at Waterloo on 16 November 1982, it was greeted by hordes of photographers, tripping over their tripods, dropping their flash guns and generally having a miserable time in the very poor light under the station roof. Again $\frac{1}{30}$ at f2.8 with a lightweight hand-held 35mm camera has produced a print of perfect depth of field and of excellent tonal graduation despite the prevailing conditions. Class 33/1 Bo-Bo No 33.113 waits to haul the unit away from the platform after the exhibition is over.

Below:
The old GWR lower quadrants at Clink Road Junction, near Frome, are situated very close to the road bridge from where this photograph was taken and only by using a 24mm wide angle lens could this view include the complete top of the gantry. Lighting on 11 January 1983 wasn't very good but $\frac{1}{500}$ at f4 on an f2 lens has proved quite adequate to cope with matters.

Above:
An attractive view of the approaches to Barnstaple taken from atop quite a steep hill. A slow climb up the grassy slopes would have been fine but I had only a few minutes to the time when the train was due! With the 35mm camera fitted with an 85mm lens swinging inconsequentially around the neck, the climb was made with seconds to spare. With the old and much heavier large format equipment this scene of Class 33/0 No 33.065 arriving at its destination with the 15.20SO Exeter St Davids-Barnstaple on 17 September 1983 would have been missed.

Right:
An attractive scene near Whiteball tunnel on 22 September 1983 with Class 50 No 50.049 *Defiance* heading a Plymouth-Paddington relief express. The exposure on a 180mm f2.8 Nikkor ED lens was $^1/_{1000}$th at f5.6. A similar exposure on an equivalent large format lens would have rendered the signals or the end of the train out of focus. To have obtained the same result the large camera user would need to 'stop down' the lens to f11 but then the resulting reduction in the shutter speed of $^1/_{250}$th would have caused the 'Hoover's' front end to blur as the beautifully clean machine was travelling at quite a pace.

Above:
Another example of a fast shutter speed being needed in order to freeze fast movement but depth of field still being necessary to keep both foreground and train in focus. Near Brentwood, Essex, on 14 May 1982, Class 312/1 Great Eastern lines outer surburban EMUs with No 312.782 leading form the 16.52 Liverpool Street-Witham.

Right:
With a weak sun facing the camera and shining through a morning mist, this photograph was, to say the least, not easy. Using an f2 Nikkor 135mm telephoto lens to cut out most of the glare from the sky, the exposure was $\frac{1}{500}$th at f5.6. The misty horizon and the station platform are both in focus to make an attractive picture of the 10.27 local to Wolverhampton — formed of a three-car BR Derby Class 108 DMU — bidding a smokey farewell to Shrewsbury on 19 August 1983.

Above:
Interiors of sheds and works often need a long exposure and frequently large camera users need to resort to the use of awkward tripods or flash if it is allowed. For this photograph, of withdrawn Waterloo & City Class 487 stock, taken underground inside the small shed at Waterloo, the camera was hand held at $\frac{1}{30}$th at f2 on a 24mm wide angle lens.

Below:
An entirely different interior but another instance where use of a 24mm wide angle lens has produced the required result. During the rail strike in the summer of 1982, HST units Nos 253.004 and 253.038 idle away their time at the bufferstops inside Penzance terminus. The wheelbarrow is being used by workmen who are taking the opportunity to make improvements to the station concourse while there are no passengers to get in the way!

Above:
On 30 June 1982 I was strolling along the sea wall at Penzance making for a new depot building at Ponsandane when, without warning due to the noise from a heavy sea, '08' shunter No 08.591 suddenly came up from behind me propelling failed 'Hoover' No 50.044 *Exeter* towards the same destination. The speedy operation of my 35mm Nikon allowed me to record this scene which would, undoubtedly, have been missed had I been using more cumbersome large format equipment.

Below:
Nothing here that a large format camera couldn't have coped with, but could the quality from a larger negative have been any better? On 1 July 1983, BR Class 56 No 56.098 passes Moira West Junction signalbox with a MGR coal train bound for Drakelow Power Station. The exposure was $\frac{1}{2000}$th at f4 on a f1.4 85mm Nikkor medium telephoto lens.

Above:
An instance where very poor light did cause problems to the number of photographers who were about with lenses no larger that f2.8. In pouring rain, newly named Class 86/2 No 86.229 *Sir John Betjeman* leaves St Pancras with a special train of SLOA stock for a run to Bedford Midland and back. Using a standard 50mm f1.4 Nikkor lens I was able to cope with the conditions without any bother, using $^1/_{500}$th at f2.8

Below:
A dull and misty morning on Holloway Bank on 31 July 1983 some half-an-hour before the sun broke through. Using metal steps to see over the high wall of the bridge. I was on the other side of the road awaiting departure from King's Cross of the newly restored and green painted Class 40 No D200 when it suddenly came into view from the other direction running 'light engine' into the terminus when I thought it was already there! Its approach sound was disguised by the Class 31 on a ballast train on the left but quick action with a very versatile Nikon FM2 camera managed to record the scene at $^1/_{1000}$th at f2.8.

Big is Beautiful

The case for the large format camera

Words and photographs by **David Wilcock**

I used to be a frustrated 'photter'. It didn't matter how I tried, none of my pictures seemed to have the sparkle that other people's pictures had. Then a friend told me. Large format. Ever since then my life has changed. No more fuzzy-round-the-edges disappointments that you get with 35mm. No more enlargements that make grain into a kind of art form. Now I feel like a new man. I can live life to the full again. Why don't you change to a large format? You'll be glad you did!

A mite too much overkill, do I hear you say? Well, perhaps such media sales-talk does oversimplify the advantages of the big camera philosophy, but after a four-year apprenticeship and perhaps 2,000 exposures with a Mamiya 6×4.5, and more recently with a Pentax 6×7, I cannot think of a single exposure I would rather have taken with my old 35mm camera.

Most present-day railway photographers who favour large format equipment will probably agree that the principal advantage is in being able to capture the working railway through the finest optical quality lenses available, and on to a film whose frame size demands only the minimum of enlargement.

Those who rarely work beyond half-plate print size may not see the point of investing in so much expensive camera gear, but the railway photographer who regards 10in×8in, 12in×10in as optimum print size, knows full well how rewarding the bigger print can be, and how the impact of a photograph can be increased dramatically by such enlargement.

It is here that the weakness of 35mm photography is exposed, for the simple logic that a negative which has to be enlarged to eight or ten times its original size, will never give the same sharp images as the negative which has only to sustain a fraction of that enlargement.

If large format enlargements are so markedly superior, why then are big cameras not more universally adopted? The answer, in a word, is cost. Following the faith of Hasselblad, Bronica, or the 6×7 Pentax, really demands that the photographer stops asking himself 'Can I afford it?' but asks instead 'Can I afford to go without it?'. Setting up even the most basic equipment (camera body, standard and short telephoto lens) in any of the three marques mentioned, can leave you with little or no change from £1,000 — but you can be confident that at this level, any inadequacies in the finished print will not be the fault of the camera.

The exponent of large format photography must however make a few sacrifices, in return for the optical excellence he will be getting. He must, for example, come to terms with a camera which is bulky and heavy to hold (at first), while his 35mm counterpart at the lineside juggles nimbly with three cameras in a frame.

Because focal length is relative to negative area, the depth of field available on large format lenses is going to be far more critical than with 35mm lenses. Similarly, the bigger apertures of 35mm lenses means the small camera man will be able to continue taking pictures in poor light, after the large format merchant has been forced to pack his camera away. Just how good the 35mm photographer's results will be in poor light at settings of $^1/_{125}$th sec at f1.4, is open to speculation, though.

Finally, if you've been used to 35mm and 36 shots-to-a-film, the idea of 10 exposures on a 120 roll may take some getting used to, but the large format photographer soon learns to be more selective with his compositions, and the temptation to 'machine-gun' an oncoming train — as often occurs in 35mm photography — doesn't arise.

The best 35mm optics — and in this category we must include Nikon, Canon and Leica — can, in some areas of performance, give the bigger cameras a close run, but in the final analysis, large format will always win the day. It's why Joddrell Bank doesn't use binoculars, too!

Above:
A very mixed bag makes up an early morning engineer's train approaching Marazion from St Erth on 1 July 1983 with Class 37 No 37.272 at the working end. Immediately behind the locomotive is a Plasser & Theurer track maintenance machine followed by a Chief Civil Engineer's Department van, a siphon G, three coal trucks and some tanks, all completed by a brake van.

Below:
Well framed by the north portals of Blea Moor Tunnel, Class 25/3 Bo-Bo No 25.323 emerges into daylight on 21 August 1983 with a Chief Civil Engineer's tunnel inspection train. On the original print it is possible to pick out every stone in the walls and very nearly every blade of grass — such is the definition from the Pentax 6cm×7cm camera fitted with a 200mm Takumar lens.

Above:
A 'Peak' in Peak country. With the onset of winter and an ETH diagram, the Class 45/1 'Peaks' became regular motive power once again over the Settle & Carlisle line at the end of 1983 taking over from the Class 31s which Holbeck had previously rostered. The arrival of No 45.114 at Blea Moor loops on 21 November 1983 was handled by a Pentax 6cm×7cm and the 200mm lens set at $\frac{1}{500}$th at f11. This combination has not only brought forward the flat-topped peak of Ingleborough, three and a half miles away, but ensures pin sharpness throughout the length of the train.

Below:
The type of 'candid' at which 35mm might excel you may think. Not a bit of it. The large format camera with its lesser depth of field has resulted in the train and driver being 'sharp' and the background being thrown nicely out of focus, thus emphasising the composition. On 28 June 1983 the driver of the first train of the day at St Erth to St Ives checks his watch before climbing into the driving cab and departing at precisely 07.20.

Above:
Having brought Class 40 No 40.155 'wrong line' from Kirkby Stephen, the driver, second man and guard of a works train watch as the Chief Civil Engineer's Department takes occupation of the Settle & Carlisle line during the repointing of Bridge No 173, near Birkett Common, on 24 August 1983. The fact that the train was 'parked' has allowed a slow shutter speed of $^1/_{60}$th second to be used with an aperture of f22, thus ensuring the depth of field on the Pentax 6cm×7cm keeps everything from the crew in the foreground to the hazy background of Mallerstang Edge in perfect focus.

Below:
Realising at the last second that the position that had been selected for this photograph would produce a house chimney protruding from the roof of the locomotive, the shutter was deliberately fired early, thus avoiding the problem. The large 6×7 negative format ensured that, despite only half the negative being used, that the overall result is still good. On 12 April 1983 Class 31/4 No 31.404 adorned with white waist stripe and 41A shed plate in the marker light panel, is rostered for train 1E33, the afternoon Carlisle-Leeds service and prepares for the Skipton stop.

Above:
Having arrived at the North Yorkshire Moors Railway from Doncaster just the day before, preserved 'Deltic' No 55.009 *Alycidon* is soon put to work and heads a train to Grosmont near Levisham on 22 August 1982. A 210mm lens fitted to a Mamiya 645 camera records the scene.

Top right:
Class 31/1s Nos 31.170 and 31.156 chunter down the old Grassington branch on a dull summer day in 1983 heading the Rylstone Tilcon block working empties from Hull. A Mamiya 645 camera was used here with Tri-X film at a setting of $^1/_{500}$th f5.6.

Bottom right:
It is seldom that a railway photograph is made as a 'straight' print from the negative. Invariably the sky will need bringing out with judicious shading or shadowed areas will need to be held back. In this photograph the unlighted section of platform beneath the canopy has been held back during exposure for the print and the sky portion has been brought out. Not an easy operation but one that is much simpler to do with the large format negative. On a sunny 23 November 1982, Class 25/2 No 25.214 brings ballast from Ribblehead Quarry through Hellifield and heads for Healy Mills.

Above:
Even as late into 1983 as 12 April, Ingleborough retains its snow topping and makes a superb backcloth to 'Whistler' No 40.196 heading train No 7E54 — a Ribblehead to Healy Mills ballast working — between Blea Moor and Ribblehead. Having run round the train the locomotive is now departing south on the up line. The scene was recorded on the Pentax 6×7 using XP1 film rated at 400ASA and the exposure on the standard 105mm Takumar lens was $^{1}/_{500}$th at f8.